Journal

Aimee Deniau

Made in the USA
Monee, IL
27 April 2021

67007248R00056